Contents

KT-226-326

What are mosquitoes?

Mosquitoes are **insects**. They have a body made up of three parts. They have six legs and two wings.

4

BUG BOOKS

Mosquito

Jill Bailey

Heinemann LIBRARY

www.heinemann.co.uk/library
Visit our website to find out more information about Heinemann Library books.

To order:
☎ Phone 44 (0) 1865 888066
🖹 Send a fax to 44 (0) 1865 314091
🖥 Visit the Heinemann Bookshop at www.heinemann.co.uk/library to browse our catalogue and order online.

First published in Great Britain by Heinemann Library, Halley Court, Jordan Hill, Oxford OX2 8EJ, part of Harcourt Education.
Heinemann is a registered trademark of Harcourt Education Ltd.

© Harcourt Education Ltd 1999, 2006
Second edition first published in paperback in 2007
The moral right of the proprietor has been asserted.

All rights reserved. No part of this publication may be reproduced, stored in a retrieval system, or transmitted in any form or by any means, electronic, mechanical, photocopying, recording, or otherwise, without either the prior written permission of the publishers or a licence permitting restricted copying in the United Kingdom issued by the Copyright Licensing Agency Ltd, 90 Tottenham Court Road, London W1T 4LP (www.cla.co.uk).

Editorial: Clare Lewis and Katie Shepherd
Design: Ron Kamen, Michelle Lisseter and Bridge Creative Services Limited
Illustrations: Alan Fraser at Pennant Illustration
Picture Research: Maria Joannou
Production: Helen McCreath

Printed and bound in China by South China Printers

13 digit ISBN 978 0 431 01834 8 (hardback)
10 09 08 07 06
10 9 8 7 6 5 4 3 2 1

13 digit ISBN 978 0 431 01898 0 (paperback)
11 10 09 08 07
10 9 8 7 6 5 4 3 2 1

British Library Cataloguing in Publication Data
Bailey, Jill
Bug Books: Mosquito - 2nd Edition
595.7'72
A full catalogue record for this book is available from the British Library.

Acknowledgements
The publishers would like to thank the following for permission to reproduce photographs:
Ardea London Ltd pp.**21** (R Gibbons), **4** (D Greenslade); Bruce Coleman Ltd pp.**20** (J Shaw), **23** (K Taylor); FLPA pp.**25** (D Gewcock), **15** (L West); Chris Honeywell p.**28**; NHPA pp.**9, 11, 14** (G Bernard), **17, 19** (S Dalton), **7** (P Parks); Oxford Scientific Films pp.**16** (R Brown), **6, 8, 10, 12, 13** (J Cooke); London Scientific Films:pp.**22; 29** (H Taylor); naturepl.com p.**18** (M Durham); Planet Earth Pictures p.**26** (A Mounter); Science Photo Library pp.**5** (T Brain), **27** (A Crump).

Cover photograph reproduced with permission of Getty Images/The Image Bank.

The publishers would like to thank Nancy Harris for her assistance in the preparation of this book.

Every effort has been made to contact copyright holders of any material reproduced in this book. Any omissions will be rectified in subsequent printings if notice is given to the publishers.

Any words appearing in the text in bold, **like this**, are explained in the Glossary

A mosquito has big eyes. It has **feelers** on its head for touching, smelling, and hearing. Baby mosquitoes are small and wriggly. They live in water.

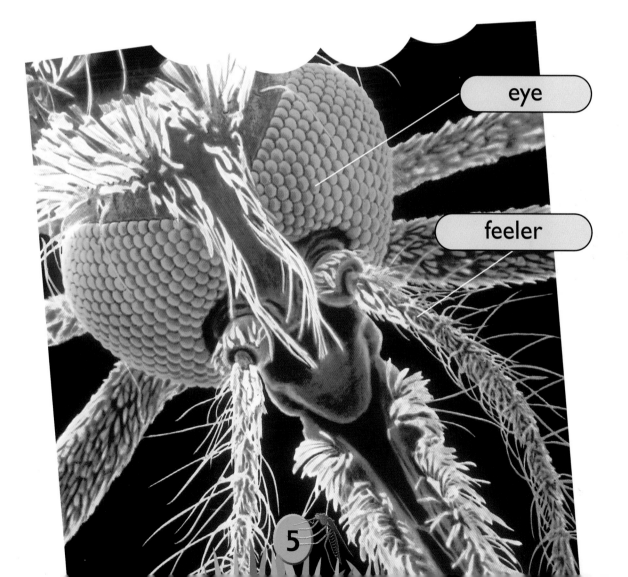

eye

feeler

What do mosquitoes look like?

Mosquitoes are very small. The common house mosquito is only as long as your little fingernail.

Mosquitoes fly in a jerky up-and-down way. Their legs hang below them as they fly. When they rest, they fold their wings.

How are mosquitoes born?

The **female** house mosquito lays lots of eggs on the surface of a small pool or puddle. The eggs float on the water.

eggs

After a few hours, the eggs **hatch**. Tiny, wriggling babies called **larvae** wriggle out and swim off.

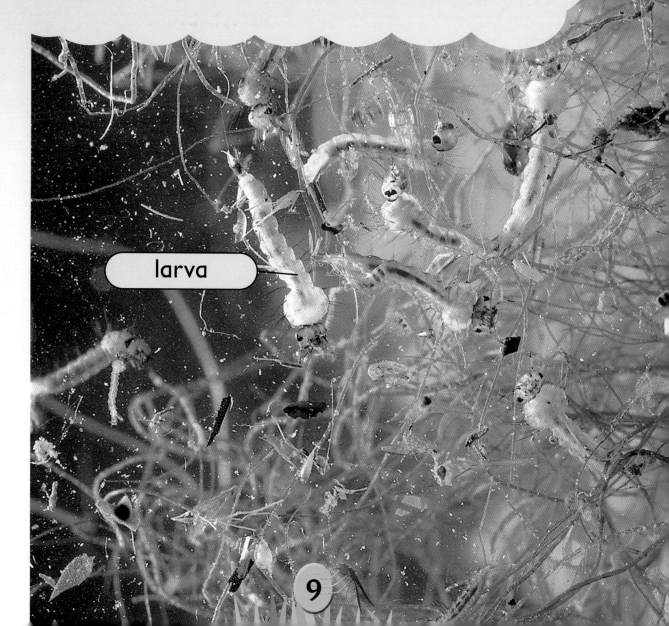

larva

How do mosquitoes grow?

The baby mosquito **larvae** hang upside-down from the water surface. They breathe in air through a long tube.

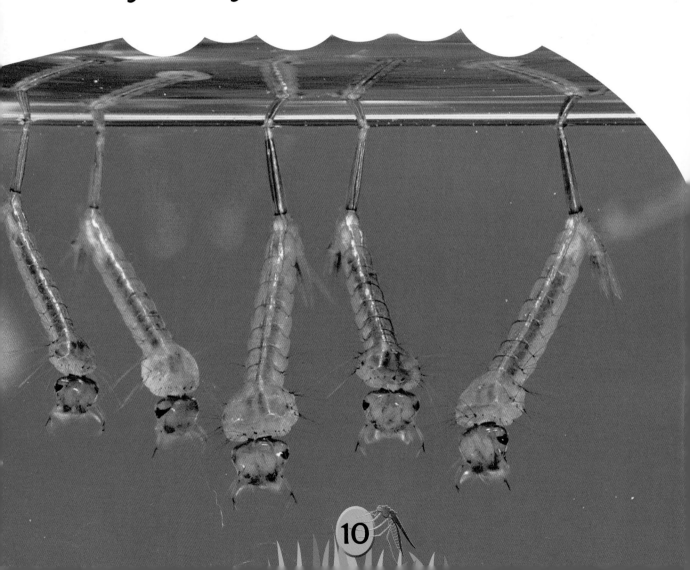

A larva's mouth is surrounded by hairs.
These hairs sweep water into its
mouth. The larva eats tiny pieces of
food that float in the water.

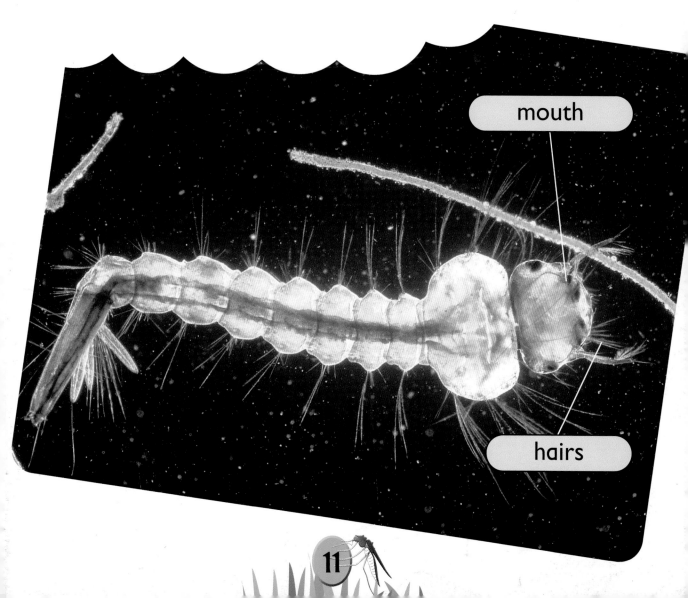

mouth

hairs

When a **larva** gets big enough it stops eating. Its head end gets very large. It is now called a **pupa**.

Inside its skin, the pupa slowly changes
into an adult mosquito. The skin splits.
The new mosquito climbs
out and flies away.

What do mosquitoes eat?

Adult mosquitoes suck up flower **nectar** through their long mouths. **Female** mosquitoes drink blood from people or animals to help them make eggs.

The female mosquito breaks the skin of an animal or person with her sharp mouth. Then she adds a juice to stop the blood **clotting** as she feeds. This juice can make the bite itch.

Which animals attack mosquitoes?

Many birds eat mosquitoes. They sometimes feed them to their babies.

Frogs, toads, rats, and mice also eat mosquitoes. Spiders catch them in their webs. Fish, water beetles, and young dragonflies eat baby mosquitoes.

How do mosquitoes move?

Adult mosquitoes can fly. A mosquito can fly a long way to look for food.

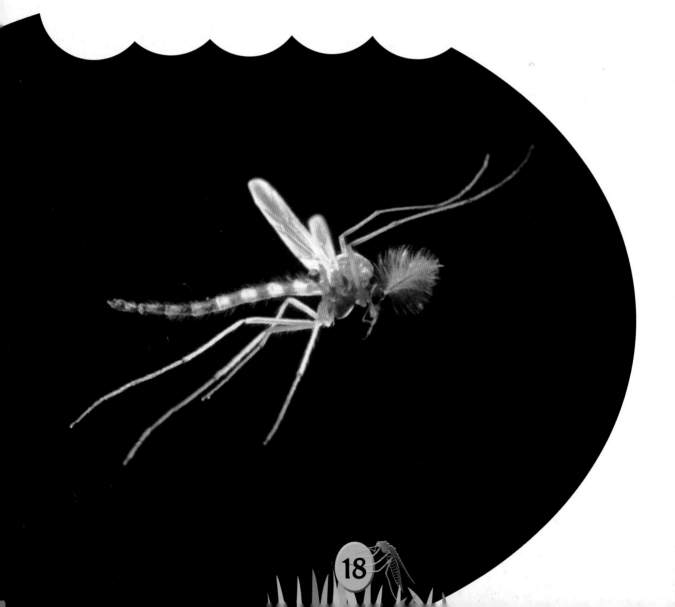

The moving wings make a whining noise.

Where do mosquitoes live?

Mosquitoes live in damp, shady places, near pools of water where their babies can live. Even small puddles are big enough for mosquito babies to live in.

Mosquitoes often come into houses and rest on walls or ceilings. They live all over the world, especially in forests in hot places.

How long do mosquitoes live?

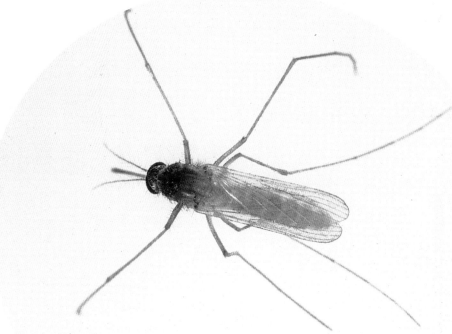

The **female** mosquitoes live longest. Sometimes they live for two or three weeks. A few mosquitoes live much longer. They sleep through the winter in houses or **hollow** trees.

These mosquitoes lay their eggs in water in the spring and then die. In less than a month there will be new adult mosquitoes. Soon they will lay their own eggs.

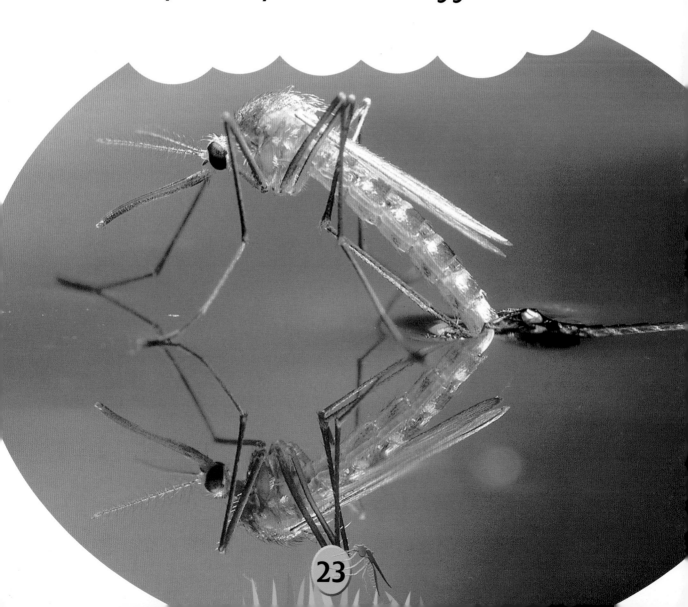

What do mosquitoes do?

Most mosquitoes hide during the day. They come out in the evening when the air is cool and damp. They look for food and other mosquitoes.

Crowds of **male** mosquitoes "dance" together to attract **females**. The males listen for the sound of the females.

How are mosquitoes special?

Mosquitoes are important food for birds and other animals. They can also cause harm. In some countries, mosquitoes spread disease, so people spray chemicals to kill them.

When a **female** mosquito sucks blood, she sometimes carries diseases from one person or animal to another. In some countries, people sleep under special nets to stop mosquitoes biting them.

Thinking about mosquitoes

Are there any large puddles or buckets of water near your home? Are there any tiny **rafts** of mosquito eggs in them?

Touch the water with a twig. Do any baby mosquito **larvae** wriggle away? If you can't find any, leave a large can of water outside in a shady place in spring or summer.

larva

Bug map

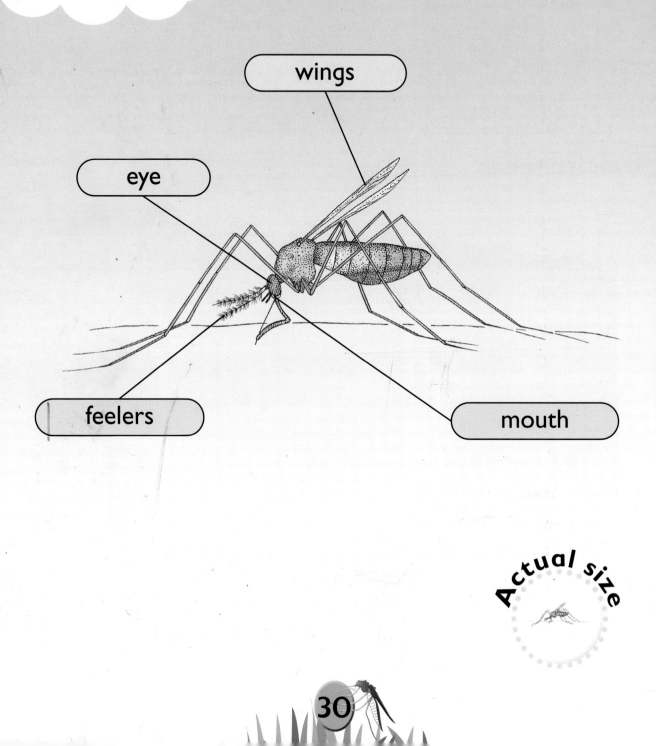

wings

eye

feelers

mouth

Actual size

Glossary

clotting when blood becomes thick, then hard, to form a plug that stops more bleeding

feelers two long bendy rods that stick out from the head of an insect. They may be used to feel, smell, or hear.

female a girl

hatch to come out of an egg

hollow a hollow tree is usually dead and the trunk is empty inside

insect a small creature with six legs

larva (more than one = larvae) the little grub that hatches from the egg

male a boy

nectar a sweet juice inside flowers

pupa (more than one = pupae) older larva. The adult mosquito grows inside it.

raft something that is flat and can float on the surface of the water

Index

More books to read

Creepy Creatures: Mosquitoes,
Sue Barraclough (Heinemann Library, 2005)